The Owl in the Woodwork

poems by

Ron Domen

Finishing Line Press
Georgetown, Kentucky

The Owl in the Woodwork

Copyright © 2017 by Ron Domen
ISBN 978-1-63534-140-9 First Edition
All rights reserved under International and Pan-American Copyright Conventions.
No part of this book may be reproduced in any manner whatsoever without written permission from the publisher, except in the case of brief quotations embodied in critical articles and reviews.

ACKNOWLEDGMENTS

Grateful acknowledgment is made to the editors of the following publications in which some of these poems (some in slightly different form) first appeared:

Black Bear Review: Asphalt Man
Earth First!: Caterpillars
Grasslands Review: Natural History
Green Fuse Poetry: Frogs
Riverwind: The Owl in the Woodwork
Slipstream: The Steel Pail
Whiskey Island Magazine: Odyssey
Wildflower: Willie B.
Wild Onions: Snow; Conception; Plaintive Music; On Buying Our Gravesites
Yarrow: Pawnee Earth Lodge

Publisher: Leah Maines

Editor: Christen Kincaid

Cover Art: Andulino (Andrea Nyilas), Budapest, Hungary

Author Photo: Kate Domen

Cover Design: Elizabeth Maines

Printed in the USA on acid-free paper.
Order online: www.finishinglinepress.com
    also available on amazon.com

Author inquiries and mail orders:
Finishing Line Press
P. O. Box 1626
Georgetown, Kentucky 40324
U. S. A.

Table of Contents

Beaver Creek 1

The Owl in the Woodwork 2

Odyssey 3

The Steel Pail 4

Frogs 5

Pawnee Earth Lodge 6

Natural History 7

Plaintive Music 8

Snow 9

Caterpillars 10

Asphalt Man 11

Conception 12

Willie B. 14

Woodsmoke 15

On Buying Our Gravesites 16

for Kate

In geological terms we all have the same measure of immortality... The days are stacked against what we think we are.

—Jim Harrison

Beaver Creek
    (for Charles Burchfield, 1893-1967)

       "...the voice of the turtle
       is heard in our land..."
       — *Song of Solomon 2:12 (KJV)*

There was a time when flowers
had thoughts and the hills heard
turtles speak of the brilliant colors
of things growing and butterfly
festivals and cricket fantasies
of red hepaticas and windblown
asters on sultry summer afternoons.
When fog lingered in late morning
light instead of escaping to Post's
Woods or Trotter's Swamp along
Little Beaver Creek you stopped
by the empty barn and sheds
at the end of an alley forsaken
and mournful as the coal mines
and coke ovens that surrounded
your small Ohio town.
You painted the hard buildings
and splendid trees with heavy
strokes of raw sienna and ocher
yellow and black never failing
to show the *strange white light*
that hovered around the edges.

The Owl in the Woodwork
(for Charles Burchfield, 1893-1967)

I soared over darkened
fields and feasted
on mice.
As the sun rose
over the hill
I plunged
into the dusky woods
to avoid the blinding
light and became lodged
between two young
white pines.
We grew together
and my eyes turned
to knots
my blood to sap
my body to wood.
Then a thunderous
splintering and buzzing
as a jagged disk
cut through me.
I hate this light.

Odyssey
    (for Charles Burchfield, 1893-1967)

The hot wind blew
and grasshoppers
bounded in waves
across dry fields.
Inside your studio
light fluttered
around the edges
of your canvas
and the stuffed
crows scowled
from their perches.
A mysterious gloom
settled on everything
as you hungered
for perpetual
summer days wandering
Ohio woodlands
and ravines
discovering clumps
of hepaticas or flocks
of blackbirds flitting
across meadows.
Outside your window
brilliant sunlight struck
with a thundering howl
and splashed over
the red barn
and white birches.

The Steel Pail
    (for my father)

The cherry wood burns
to a pile of gray-white
ashes but not before
it fills the room
with the sweet smell
of itself and releases
to the fire blues
oranges and reds locked
somewhere inside.
As a boy you climbed
the cherry tree
now neatly stacked
in the woodpile
and collected the tart
dark red fruit
in a gray steel pail.
But no matter
what you gathered
the path always led back
to that three-roomed
miner's shack with bitter
and pungent smells
of kerosene lamps
and woodsmoke
to a mother who would
not talk and a father
who left bloody coal-flecked
phlegm in a coffee can
next to the potbelly stove.

Frogs

Radioactive leopard
frogs born from toxic
uterine mud behind
Oak Ridge National
Laboratory leap
like lambent fugitives
down highway sixty-two
to become radiant
amphibian clots
plastered on tires
of cars and trucks
dashing through the night.

Pawnee Earth Lodge
> *"And the noise of the geese
> remembers the promise."*
> — Pawnee Legend

In a Chicago museum I enter
a replica of a lodge and feel
the calm of hewn timber
clods of dirt and grass
the smoothness of lost
corners and sharp angles.
A firepit lies below a hole
in the domed roof and in
the west under the hanging
sacred bundle which contains
things of the earth a buffalo
skull sits upon an altar.
This house is not more than
a bubble on the surface of nature.
Where does one start
and the other end?
The door always faces east
to catch the rising sun
and the fire is in the center.

Natural History
    (for M.B.)

We walked through the Pharaoh's tomb
brought to Chicago three thousand
years after masons cut the massive
stone blocks out of the earth.
Next to his two mummified children
we talked of the burden of being
part-time fathers and felt the weight
of disagreeable compromises.
In the Hall of Mammals we sat
on a wooden bench and spoke
about your upcoming surgery
and the relief it might bring while
the two man-eating lions of Tsavo
stuffed and posed glared
from glass enclosed natural splendor.

Plaintive Music

On that day in waning winter
as the sunrise spread red-orange
and purple like a bruise only

the brightest star Sirius could still
be seen pulsating like the dot
of heart on the sonogram

of our unborn child wrapped
in ariled darkness before it too
disappeared in the morning light.

Now in the last days of summer
newly hatched cicadas brown-red
as blood clots rise from grounded

dormancy on journeys marked
by liturgical drones until their bronzed
chitinous skin becomes too tight

to hold such plaintive music
and splits to leave behind empty
hard-shelled wombs.

Snow

on this first morning
of the year and eleven inches
already cover the ground.
Only a few weeks ago the wild
geese ran in waves across
the field in front
of the children who thought
they could herd them into flight.
But the geese stayed until
the lake began to freeze
then like a frustrated spouse
lifted off south in a burst
of flapping wings
and clamorous honks.

Caterpillars

The fog finally lugs
itself from the meadow
leaving behind Red-winged
Blackbirds to ramble
through grasses
and hardwood saplings
heads bobbing
as they peck for bugs
in brown dirt.
Clusters of white
flowered Yarrow
fill gaps between
the road and useless
fence the rotting
posts returning
to soil like the old
man who farmed
this land.
Down the road
yellow Caterpillars
belch and snort
from their smoky
engines as they claim
and reshape these fields.

Asphalt Man
   (for Loren Eiseley, 1907-1977)

The dead yield their secrets
through layers of dirt
and flesh turned to ash
and white bony skulls
with empty sockets
that no longer see.
The bones warn us that
only confusion lies
in mass-produced daydreams
that truth is not reached
by sleek and fast highways
where asphalt man blindly
walks the road laid
down by the dead.
But the dead tell us
to look to the past
to see inside ourselves
for the future.

Conception

It is important to know the stories
that surround our conception.
But leave out the part about the hormone
surge that expands the cumulus cells
surrounding the zona pellucida
and prepares the egg for fertilization.
I would rather know if there was passionate
love-making in the back seat of a Ford
at a drive-in movie the rolled up windows
made opaque from your steamy breaths.

And don't go into detail how sperm
must fight their way through fibrous
macromolecules in cervical mucus
to get to fallopian tube fimbria
where the egg awaits fertilization.
Tell me about the gibbous moon
that rose above the swell of waves
on your honeymoon beach
and like sea turtles hatching
out of the sand and making their way
back to salt water I too
started my journey there on the sand.

And don't use medical terms like capacitation
or hyperactivation to describe how sperm
must penetrate the zona pellucida
in order to fertilize the egg.
I want to know the details of how
the fog-laden air hung lanuginous
and misty in the park's twilight
and dew on the grass mixed
with the lustrous sweat on your bodies.

And if you start to tell me about
sperm crossing the egg's equatorial
segment and membrane fusion followed
by cleavage and embryo implantation
I will wonder about the outside drone
of traffic mingling with the radio's music
in your bedroom as shadows from streetlights
streaked across the bed and the sound of me
came like the rustle of clothes dropped
to the floor around your feet.

Willie B.

Captured from lowland
forest under African skies
where you played free
and learned things gorilla
to a small cement room
in the Atlanta Zoo.
Twenty-seven years
not allowed sunshine
shade of tree
squish of earth
between toes.
Your world a carousel
of faces.
A new exhibit
with grass and sky
remote and hostile
to your hesitant steps.

Woodsmoke

> *"For my days are consumed like smoke…"*
> — Psalm 102:3 (KJV)

A cold November rain studded
with flurries strips the final
skin of leaves and lays bare
the bones of trees to bring it all
back to stark simplicity once
again like this oak library
table where I write that was carried
by the B&O from Pittsburgh
to my great grandmother's Ohio
parlor almost a hundred years
ago this winter when my father
and I strip off the dark aged
varnish and sand smooth
the deep grained honey-colored
wood until the accumulated
crust of a century gathers
around our feet and the wood
dust covers our clothes and sticks
tenaciously to our hair.
Not until my father lays down
a new skin of varnish caressing
the oil deep into the raw oak
with his bare bony hands
does it finally come back
to its pure and marvelous
and ordinary self like the clean
smell of woodsmoke that comes
out of nowhere from an unknown
hearth on a winter day
when I breathe deep drafts of it
into my lungs until it becomes
part of my own steamy breath
visible in the frost-laden air.

On Buying Our Gravesites

> *The living know that they will die,*
> *but the dead know nothing...*
> — Ecclesiastes 9:5 (NRSV)

Snow begins to fall once again
on this windswept knoll along
the Lehigh River where the black

bony trees and dark gravestones
dot the slope of Nisky Hill
and the crisscross tracks

of small animals about their early
morning business are visible
in the whiteness.

We stand on the eastern portion
of the northern one-half of lot
two in section G and survey

the nearby family names etched
in granite where our corporeal selves
will huddle among oaks and sycamores

in shared hallowed dirt
the affairs of earth like Cezanne's
black clock with no hands.

Additional Acknowledgments

"Frogs" also appeared in *Cattle Bones & Coke Machines: An Anthology of Poems Examining the Impact of Humanity on the Earth's Energy Systems*, Smiling Dog Press, Maple City, Michigan, 1995.

"Beaver Creek" appeared in *Voices of Cleveland: A Bicentennial Anthology of Poems by Contemporary Cleveland Poets*, Cleveland State University Poetry Center, Cleveland, Ohio, 1996; and in, *I Have My Own Song For It: Modern Poems of Ohio*, edited by Elton Glaser and William Greenway, The University of Akron Press, Akron Series in Poetry, Akron, Ohio, 2002.

"Odyssey" also appeared in *Cityscape*, edited by Bonnie Jacobson and Leonard Trawick; a publication in the "Poetry: Mirror of the Arts Series," sponsored by the Poets' League of Greater Cleveland, Cleveland, Ohio, 1996; and, was staged and performed by actors at the Cleveland Museum of Art, Cleveland, Ohio, on June 5, 1996, as part of the Cleveland Museum of Art's special exhibition *Transformations in Cleveland Art, 1796-1946*.

"Conception" also appeared in *Hektoen International: A Journal of Medical Humanities*, Volume 2, Issue 3; Fall 2010 (Published by the Hektoen Institute of Medicine, Chicago, Illinois).

"Plaintive Music" also appeared in *Hektoen International: A Journal of Medical Humanities*, Volume 4, Issue 3; Fall 2012 (Published by the Hektoen Institute of Medicine, Chicago, Illinois).

My thanks to the poets Christopher Bursk, Patricia Goodrich, Cortney Davis, and the late Len Roberts, for help and encouragement along the way, and to the Virginia Center for the Creative Arts for a fellowship that provided me space and solitude in which some of these poems were written or conceived.

Special thanks to my wife, Kate, for her critical reading of my work, and her never-ending support and encouragement.

Ron Domen is currently a Professor of Pathology, Medicine, and Humanities at the Penn State University College of Medicine/Penn State Hershey Medical Center, Hershey, Pennsylvania. From 2005-2013 he was the Associate Dean for Graduate Medical Education at Penn State. He was an elected member of the Doctors Kienle Center for Humanistic Medicine at the Penn State College of Medicine for ten years. He is a nationally recognized expert in transfusion medicine and has also been active on the national level in addressing medical education and ethical issues in pathology, transfusion medicine, and transplantation, and has also published in these areas. He was a fellow at the Virginia Center for the Creative Arts (poetry) and has been writing poetry for many years and has numerous poems published in anthologies and small press magazines including: *Whiskey Island Magazine, Yarrow, Slipstream, Riverwind, Earth First!, Slant, Grasslands Review, Green Fuse*, and others. He also served as the poetry editor for The *International Journal of Healthcare & Humanities*.

Dr. Domen was born in rural Dennison, Ohio, in Tuscarawas County, and grew up in industrial Warren, Ohio. Before graduating from Youngstown State University he worked as a gas station attendant and auto-mechanic, a laborer in a steel mill, a veterinary assistant, and a hospital orderly. For various logical and illogical reasons he decided to pursue his medical studies in Guadalajara, Mexico where he graduated from the Universidad Autonoma de Guadalajara with the MD degree in 1975. He lives in Hershey, PA with his wife, Kate, and their two dogs: Darby, a Westie, and Bailey, a rescued Schnorkie.

www.ingramcontent.com/pod-product-compliance
Lightning Source LLC
LaVergne TN
LVHW041524070426
835507LV00012B/1809